Table of Contents

Chapter 1

THE HISTORY OF FASHION

People have used clothing to show off their personal style since ancient times. But clothing wasn't always about fashion. Clothing could reveal social status. Clothing could also signal membership in a certain culture or group.

Ancient Egyptians made fabric from flax, a plant fiber. They used the fabric to make tunics, robes, short-sleeved shirts, and pleated skirts. Many women filled out their wardrobes with draped dresses made of white or unbleached fabric. Both men and women wore braided leather sandals.

Ancient Romans wore togas. These one-piece wool garments were draped loosely around the shoulders and down the body. Over time, Roman women began wearing long, pleated dresses called stolas.

Ancient Egyptian artwork shows the clothing of the time.

Fabric and color choice could show a person's class standing in ancient China. The Han people wore yi, long tunics tied with sashes, and narrow skirts called chang. Women's skirts would reach their ankles or the floor, while men's skirts reached their knees. The clothing of wealthy people usually were made of silk and were painted colors such as red and green. Other people wore clothing made from hemp or ramie, both strong fibers.

Red silk clothing was common among wealthy people in ancient China.

Searchlight BOOKS™

My Style

My Fierce Fashion

Lakita Wilson

Lerner Publications ◆ Minneapolis

Lerner Publications Company
An imprint of Lerner Publishing Group, Inc.
241 First Avenue North
Minneapolis, MN 55401 USA

For reading levels and more information, look up this title at www.lernerbooks.com.

Main body text set in Adrianna Regular.
Typeface provided by Chank.

Library of Congress Cataloging-in-Publication Data

Names: Wilson, Lakita, author.
Title: My fierce fashion / Lakita Wilson.
Description: Minneapolis : Lerner Publications, 2022. | Series: Searchlight books - my style | Includes bibliographical references and index. | Audience: Ages 8–11 | Audience: Grades 4–6 | Summary: "Readers learn fascinating fashion history and how to put together fresh, comfortable outfits they feel confident in. From cool clothes to fashion icons, this fun style guide has it all"— Provided by publisher.
Identifiers: LCCN 2020017742 | ISBN 9781728404226 (lib. bdg.) | ISBN 9781728423715 (pbk.) | ISBN 9781728418650 (eb pdf)
Subjects: LCSH: Fashion—History.
Classification: LCC GT511 .W55 2020 | DDC 391.009—dc23

LC record available at https://lccn.loc.gov/2020017742

Manufactured in the United States of America
1-48480-48994-7/14/2021

Clothing made by people from Mali

Clothing in Africa

In western Africa, clothing was historically used for communicating history and stories. People of the Mali Empire wore hand-printed cloths called bògòlanfini, or mud cloths. On the cloths, they arranged symbols that had meanings and communicated tribal stories. The language of the cloths was passed down from mother to daughter. Men were responsible for weaving the fabric, and women dyed it.

The Yoruba people of western Africa used symbols in dyed clothing to represent their culture's history, folktales, and legends. They used adire textile (tie and dye) as early as the twelfth century. The cloth was tied so the indigo (blue) dye they used would resist the dye in places and create patterns.

▲

THESE MEN WEAR TRADITIONAL
YORUBA CLOTHING.

The people of southern Uganda were some of the first people to create environmentally friendly clothing. The people had so much respect for the Mutaba tree that they found a way to harvest its bark cloth for loincloth and skirts without harming the tree. Modern clothing manufacturers borrow from this tradition by making clothing from recycled products.

Many other groups of people have a history of distinct and innovative clothing. Clothing and fashion have changed and evolved throughout history.

Close-up of an African textile made from tree bark

Chapter 2

FASHION TRENDS

Some styles of clothing and accessories are popular at specific times. Some of these fashion trends last only months, while others last for many years. Fashion trends can also come and go, becoming popular in more than one period.

In the US in the 1920s, fashion trends led to clothes being designed to give women more freedom. Corsets became less popular, while shorter hemlines and shorter hair became more popular. Many women in the 1950s wanted to show off an hourglass figure. So they wore full skirts and tight tops. Music and social movements inspired fashion in the 1960s and 1970s. Then many people wore bell-bottom pants and flowing jumpsuits.

Boys show their style in the 1980s.

That's a Fact!

Fashion is influenced by many factors. But did you know fashion was influenced by World War II (1939–1945)? During the war, many women went to work and started wearing pants. They also began wearing shorts because of a shortage of fabric. Less fabric is needed to make shorts than pants.

A man and woman wear pants in the 1940s.

Many people look to social media for fashion inspiration.

During the 1980s and 1990s, people turned to supermodels and celebrities for fashion ideas. But by the 2010s, social media accounts from all over the world were inspiring new fashions. Celebrities posted photos of themselves wearing off-shoulder tops, skater skirts, skinny jeans, and cute bags. Their followers scrambled to copy their favorite looks. Social media allowed even those who weren't famous to show off their styles. Kids created their own fashion platforms that showed off their looks and trends.

Eco-Friendly Clothing

For many people, deciding what to wear involves choosing colors, fabrics, or comfort. Others are looking for brands that also show their love for the environment. Factories often use harmful chemicals to produce clothing. These chemicals and other dangerous waste can seriously hurt our environment and the people who produce them.

Some clothing brands are using more eco-friendly materials, like hemp and bamboo, to create clothing. These options, called sustainable clothing, are made to

Wearing eco-friendly or recycled clothing helps create less waste.

SOME CLOTHES ARE MADE FROM ORGANIC COTTON, AN ECO-FRIENDLY MATERIAL.

be worn multiple times before needing to be washed. This helps reduce the amount of water we use washing clothes.

Other clothing companies are making their production more eco-friendly. Some grow organic cotton without using harmful chemicals, and recycle clothing and natural materials. Some clothing brands even plant trees for every piece of clothing they sell. They replenish the resources they've used.

Celebrities are also turning to eco-friendly fashion. The Green Carpet Challenge was started in 2010 when Livia Firth, founder and creative director of Eco-Age, wore sustainable gowns for red carpet events to show that clothing could be both eco-friendly and glamourous. She's continued to wow celebrities and fans with her red carpet looks. In 2015, she walked the red carpet wearing a gown made entirely of recycled plastic bottles.

Livia Firth wears a gown made from reclaimed fabric at the Oscars in 2010.

Style Icon

When she was four years old, Cecilia Cassini of Encino, California, cut up her sister's dress and pinned it to fit herself. She told her parents that she could do an even better job if she had a sewing machine. Two years later, her parents bought one for her. Cecilia started designing her own looks. By the age of twelve, Cecilia was selling her clothes in boutiques. She also starred in her own fashion TV show.

Cecilia poses for a photo at the 2011 Young Hollywood Awards.

In 2017, actor Emma Watson wore a black chiffon and silk dress made entirely of organic materials while promoting her new movie *Beauty and the Beast*. Other stars and world-famous designers like Gucci and Armani have added sustainable gowns to the red carpet to show that clothing can be both eco-friendly and stylish.

At a New York fundraiser in 2016, Emma Watson wears a gown made out of recycled plastic bottles.

Chapter 3

WARDROBE BASICS

To create your own unique fashions, start with the basics. A capsule wardrobe is your collection of essential items. These are clothes, such as jeans and basic tees, that won't go out of style and can be worn every season of the year. Starting your capsule wardrobe is simple. First, figure out what you love to wear and what you don't. Then learn the art of mixing and matching.

Keeping your closet organized helps you know what clothes you have in your wardrobe.

Go through your clothes, shoes, and accessories, and sort them into three piles. Organize your items into a *love* pile, a *maybe* pile, and a *gotta go* pile. Sort your love pile by tops, bottoms, and accessories. Then arrange those items by color and place them back in your closet or dresser.

Set your *maybe* pile aside for a few weeks. Think about whether you should keep or ditch the items in it. You can donate the *gotta go* pile to a charity or to a place that sells secondhand items, such as a thrift shop. But if the clothes are stained or not wearable, ask a parent's permission to bring them to a recycling center. Some cities have recycling centers with a spot to drop off clothes to be recycled. Recycling clothes helps the environment by saving energy needed to make new materials.

DONATION

DONATING CLOTHES INSTEAD OF THROWING THEM AWAY IS GOOD FOR THE ENVIRONMENT.

Completing Your Wardrobe

Once you've cleaned out your closet, you'll have a clearer idea of what's missing from your wardrobe. Then you can build up your wardrobe over time. Make a checklist of things you want to buy to fill in the gaps. When going to stores or consignment shops, stick to your list and budget. Try to include only things you truly need or things that you will love for a long time.

Friends and family make great shopping partners and can help you find cool clothes.

That's a Fact!

In the United States, the average person owns seven pairs of blue jeans. That's one for every day of the week! Levi Strauss & Co. released their first blue jeans in 1873. Levi's is one of the most popular brands of jeans. Although a modern pair costs much more, the first pair of Levi's jeans sold for six dollars' worth of gold dust, according to one story.

A pair of Levi's jeans

Another way to make your clothes feel fresh is to mix and match your outfits. Try putting your clothing together in different pairings, using different accessories. Revisit your closet each season. This will help you refresh it or get rid of things that don't fit, or are no longer your style.

Chapter 4

CREATING YOUR OWN LOOKS

Keeping up with fashion trends can be fun. But you don't have to let other people decide what you should wear. With a bit of confidence, you can pull off any outfit, even one you've created on your own.

Ask permission from a parent or guardian to search for apps and websites that let you design your own looks. Some sites will help you explore fabrics, textures, cuts, and accessories.

Other sites allow you to design entire wardrobes. You can also check out your local library or classes offered by your school to learn about making your own creations. Some libraries have sewing machines, and some schools have sewing classes.

YOU CAN ALSO FIND CLOTHING INSPIRATION BY SEEING WHAT PEOPLE AROUND YOU WEAR.

Colored pens, markers, and paper are some tools you can use to design clothes.

Design Purpose and Inspiration

Before designing your own wardrobe, think about the purpose of the clothes. Are you creating looks to wear to school or just for fun? Do you want to create a formal piece of clothing or something casual? Next, find something that inspires you. You can look online, around your home, in nature, or at photos taken at glamorous events. Try to sketch your design first. Think about how colors and patterns work together. Rework your sketch through drawing or fashion apps until you're happy with the final design.

Remember that fashion changes over time. So will your personal style. That's fine! With these tips and tricks, you can keep learning about and updating your fashion.

While choosing outfits, pick clothing that you feel comfortable and happy in.

Fashion Hack

Decorating your clothing with pins printed with fun sayings or pictures can be a playful way to express yourself. Start by collecting pins that show off your favorite hobbies and interests, make you laugh, or send an important message. You can ask a friend or relative if they have any pins they'd be willing to share. Or you can buy affordable pins at a thrift store. Then simply attach the pins to your clothes or a vest however you like. Just be careful not to poke yourself with the pins. When you're done, you're ready to show off your fun look!

Glossary

accessory: an item, such as a hair clip or sunglasses, added to something else to make it more useful or attractive

designer: a person who draws and makes plans for creating something

sandals: light, open shoes with straps

secondhand: having had a previous owner

sustainable: using a resource in such a way that the resource is not used up or damaged

textile: a cloth made by weaving or knitting

tie and dye: a method of dying fabric in patterns by tying parts of it to shield it from the dye

trend: the latest style

Learn More

Clothing Facts for Kids
   https://kids.kiddle.co/Clothing

Fashion
   https://kids.britannica.com/kids/article/fashion/390746

Plumley, Amie Petronis, and Andria Lisle. *Sewing School Fashion Design: Make Your Own Wardrobe with Mix-and-Match Projects Including Tops, Skirts & Shorts*. North Adams, MA: Storey, 2019.

Ware, Lesley. *How to Be a Fashion Designer*. New York: DK, 2018.

What Do You Wear
   https://easyscienceforkids.com/all-about-what-do-you-wear/

Wilson, Lakita. *My Cool Jewelry*. Minneapolis: Lerner Publications, 2022.

Index

Photo Acknowledgments

Image credits: ingehogenbijl/Shutterstock.com, p. 5; loonger/E+/Getty Images, p. 6; john images/Moment/Getty Images, p. 7; Ajibola Fasola/Shutterstock.com, p. 8; ChWeiss/ Shutterstock.com, p. 9; Roman Nerud/Shutterstock.com, p. 11; H. Armstrong Roberts/ Retrofile RF/Getty Images, p. 12; Cristian Dina/Shutterstock.com, p. 13; neenawat khenyothaa/ Shutterstock.com, p. 14; Tero Vesalainen/Shutterstock.com, p. 15; Jaguar PS/Shutterstock .com, p. 16; Kathy Hutchins/Shutterstock.com, p. 17; Ovidiu Hrubaru/Shutterstock.com, p. 18; Mari Nevich/Shutterstock.com, p. 20; Veja/Shutterstock.com, p. 21; Prostock-studio/ Shutterstock.com, p. 22; Nor Gal/Shutterstock.com, p. 23; Daniel Grill/Getty Images, p. 24; Thomas Barwick/Getty Images, p. 26; Jeffrey Coolidge/Stone/Getty Images, p. 27; Rohappy/ Shutterstock.com, p. 28.

Cover: Head over Heels/Shutterstock.com; Kiselev Andrey Valerevich/Shutterstock.com; Mark Nazh/Shutterstock.com.